INCREASE YOUR CASH FLOW

Serviced Accommodation

Julian Businge

Published in Great Britain by Greatness University Publishers
Website: www.greatness-university.com
ISBN: 978-1-9999494-6-4
ISBN: 1999949463

DEDICATION

This book is dedicated to my husband Dr Patrick Businge with whom I started my business and he inspires me to continue the journey to live my dream of helping others. To my beloved children Princess Stella and Prince Eric Businge who motivate me on a daily basis with their love. Thank you all for allowing me to make a positive contribution to society.

Julian Businge

CONTENTS

ACKNOWLEDGMENTS

There are many people who have made this book possible. Their knowledge, inspiration, and dedication has made my dream of being a published author become true. I am so grateful for you all.

I am thankful to my husband Dr Patrick Businge who has played a key role it publishing this book. I don't know what I would do without him as he has spent countless hours working on the layout of this book so that it is accessible to all of my readers.

A special thanks to my mother Mrs Lucy Sabiiti, my sisters, and family members for believing in me. They have been a source of support and encouragement to me.

My sincere thanks to my coach and mentor Theresa Lawrie Ashton. I have become who I am because of her tireless support and belief in me.

Julian Businge

FOREWORD

It's a pleasure to be asked to say a few words about Julian, her amazing business, and her first book of many. I am proud to be called her coach and most definitely her friend.

Julian is a passionate businesswoman. She inspires many to create the life they wish to achieve with the strategy of Service Accommodation.

Opening Peace Apartments and then the Peace Property Education business while raising her family is an awesome achievement. With all the skills that Julian shares with her clients they are achieving amazing things.

I look forward to be supporting her and working as a team to enable Peace Apartments and Peace Property Education to continue to grow so as to create many more successful property businesses. Julian you are inspiring.

Theresa Lawrie-Ashton
Your coach and friend

INTRODUCTION

My Story

Before going on serviced accommodation, it is important that I share my story with you. I was born and raised in Uganda. I came to England, UK to join my husband and start our family. When I first arrived in England, I worked mostly night shifts in both the children and elderly healthcare sectors.

Before we go further, let me ask you one question: has life ever hit you hard that it took you 3 steps backwards before you could make a comeback? This is what happened to me in July 2016 when I lost my job. My boss fired me on the day I was traveling to Uganda for my annual leave. She called me to her office and told me that I didn't have to come back to work after my holiday because of a few reasons one of them being that she was restructuring her company…. I accepted the news and went on to tell my family who could not believe it. I was confused and didn't know what to do next and where to start. We were catching our flight in a few hours so I couldn't start searching for jobs immediately.

I have always believed and felt that nothing just happens: It was my time to maximize my potential. I then made a decision with my husband that when we returned back from Uganda, I was never going to look for another job but concentrate on the small investment of serviced apartments using the rent to rent property strategy we had started building the previous year. Implementing this decision and strategy involved a lot of patience, hard work and sacrifice but it has all been worth it.

Today, we have over 20 serviced apartments in Luton and looking to grow nationally and globally. My dreams have become a reality. I have had an opportunity to be trained and mentored by the leading legend of motivational speaking Mr. Les Brown. I have resolved to dedicate myself to helping others by using my own life an as example that a lot of possibilities lie ahead of us and only you have the key to unlock your potential.

I now have lots of time for my family and I am able to contribute positively in different ways to the community. When I worked night shifts, I was always half asleep and awake. While working nights was convenient in a way, I missed out on a lot of my children' activities as I would be sleeping during the day. I now feel good about myself as I have time to see my children go to bed in the night. And my biggest win is 'No Boss'. It's possible to overcome just about anything if you have a dream and believe it's possible. According to me, serviced accommodation is the easiest gateway to property investing.

A Walk through the Chapters

Thank you for choosing to read my book which is about the journey I have travelled in my serviced accommodation business. You might be asking yourself, 'what is serviced accommodation?' This is the subject of this study. I have written it for you so that you can start taking ACTION to achieve your financial goals.

As you read this book, you will discover that I have made mistakes in my business. You too will make mistakes along the way. It is my hope that by the end of this book, you will learn from them and develop the skills necessary to manage them better next time.

So, in chapter 1, you will discover what service accommodation is and how it is different from hotels. In chapter 2, you will have a chance to consider investing in serviced accommodation and what it will take you. In chapter 3, I will present you with models of investing in serviced accommodation and you will decide which one suits you best. In chapter 4, you will explore the relationship between serviced accommodation and rent to rent. In chapter 5, you will taste the nitty gritty of running a serviced accommodation on a daily basis. We will then shift to increasing your cash flow in chapter 6, how to invest in property in chapter 7, and the ways you could secure mortgages in chapter 8. In the final chapters 9 and 10, we will reflect on what might be stopping you and give you the secrets to succeed in your journey to increasing the cash flow using serviced accommodation. Enjoy your reading and feel free to contact me at **peaceproperty@yahoo.co.uk** should you have any questions.

CHAPTER 1

SERVICED ACCOMMODATION

Serviced Accommodation

As the demand for short term lets is high, professionals are looking for the privacy and flexibility of having their own apartments. Contractors are attracted by accommodation closer to their current jobs. Holiday makers are looking for more interesting alternatives to standard hotels. The great news is that online platforms such as Airbnb and Booking.com have taken all the hassle out of linking up short term guests with savvy investors who provide attractive short term lets. What does this mean for you?

For me, it means I have the opportunity to make thousands of money in extra profit using the serviced accommodation model. This is why I have written this book so that you are are able to learn from my journey.

Sometimes referred to as serviced apartments, serviced accommodation refers to fully furnished apartments which are made available to guests for short and long term stays. Serviced Apartments offer the guest services and amenities like traditional hotels but with added convenience, space, and comfort and privacy like at home. One can enjoy the feeling like living at home while travelling somewhere else. So, what can you expect from a serviced apartment?

- A fully equipped kitchen with dishwasher, fridge, microwave and washing machine

- One or more individual bedrooms designated as sleeping area

- All utilities like the water and electricity are included

- Bathroom with all the amenities

- Weekly or daily housekeeping service

- Living space

- Television

- WiFi

In addition, some of the serviced apartments include access to the gym, restaurants, and meeting rooms. Indeed, serviced apartments offer facilities that give guests the feeling of staying at home. If you were faced with the choice between staying in a serviced accommodation or hotel, here are tips to help you decided.

Serviced accommodation versus hotels?

Comfort

Rather than taking a room in a hotel when staying in a new location, some people prefer their home comforts. Serviced accommodation provides them with this as they give them comforts such as en suite bedrooms and studios fully equipped modern kitchens, internet, entertainment, and private telephone line. These amenities help them become accustomed to their new surroundings.

Many companies are now choosing to rent serviced accommodation for their employees. The reason for this is that they are a little cheaper and a more pleasant option than renting hotel rooms. This is a win-win situation for these companies because not only are they saving money on hotel costs, they are also giving their staff more comfort.

Cheaper Rates

In the current economic climate, companies are looking at cutting costs and serviced accommodation offers a cheaper alternative to hotels. Serviced apartments are typically 25% to 30% cheaper than hotels globally. Many companies have to increasingly cover the accommodation requirements for contractors and employees working on projects running over many months, it can add a significant saving to use serviced accommodation. In most serviced apartments there's free Wi-Fi compared to some hotels who charge internet connection which is much needed for most peoples' work.

Serviced Apartments are actually cheaper than hotels because they do not have extra services such as daily cleaning, a fully operational restaurant and room service. Even more so, when considering that sharing apartments is very common, because of the space, extra beds could be included when requested for. This can potentially cut the costs in half. An apartment offers the opportunity to do some laundry and eat what they choose to cook rather than what is on the menu as it's a self catering service.

Flexibility

The current economic climate has meant that companies are moving employees around on a more short-term basis as opposed to committing to long-term assignments, as short term assignments can be terminated more easily. So, instead of having to commit to a 6 or 12 month tenancy, companies are opting to use serviced accommodation due to the flexibility that it offers. No one is tied to having a contract as it's more of a 'pay as you go' system. If you are a company interested in finding these kinds of apartments for your team and are struggling, feel free to contact me.

Convenience

The ability for guests to do what they want when they want means they are not restricted as they would be in a hotel. So they can clean their clothes as most serviced apartments are fully furnished with: a washing machine in, make breakfast or dinner, have a snack, or make a cup of coffee without having to wait endlessly for room service.

Globalisation

Due to globalisation there has been a shift in employment methods and patterns. The proliferation of contractors in virtually every sector of the job market means that there are more project workers, managers, specialists, and many others that are being moved between locations to fulfil different key business functions for varying amounts of time. This has given rise to 'a home from home' for these people who can work in a specific location from one week through to a number of months depending on their needs.

Serviced accommodation serves this need better than traditional hotels.

Cooking

Serviced apartments include a fully equipped kitchen. This means means guests can cook anytime they want! With this option they are able to save money, as well as stay healthier. If a guest or their loved one suffers from food allergies or a specific condition that calls for a strict diet, having the opportunity to cook themselves is a great advantage. Service apartment rather than traditional hotels is what people are looking for due to the many amenities.

Security

Serviced apartments are often located in safe neighborhoods and are within an enclosed facility. For added safety, some have CCTV. Some have a 24 hour reception service commonly known as a meet and greet team is also available in case a guest has any issues or need special assistance. This will enable guests to have peace of mind during their stay.

Holiday lets or serviced apartment?

You have a chance to look at the different between serviced accommodation and hotels. You might be asking, is there a difference between a serviced accommodation and a holiday let? A holiday home or let is basically a home, cottage, house or property used for vacations. Holiday makers who are the main users of these homes can rent and run them as if it were their own home for the duration of their stay. This kind of accommodation is common for holiday-makers and is a good option for independent travellers who like to be in charge: you decide on times to come and go, prepare your own meals and change rooms as you wish. Traditionally, travellers who enjoy a private peaceful getaway will always go for a holiday home.

A service apartment comes with more and that is why it is termed as a home away from home. It basically is a fully furnished apartment available for both short and long term stays, allows you for space and privacy.

Julian Businge

CHAPTER 2

INVESTING IN SERVICED ACCOMMODATION

Who can invest in serviced apartments?

Investment in serviced apartments is growing at a fast rate over any other property investment strategy. This property strategy is ideal for various kinds of people depending on what they are looking to achieve financially now and in the future. It is ideal for people who are looking:

- To raise finance or deposit for their properties

- For financial freedom

- An alternative career

- To become debt free .

Serviced accommodation is also ideal for:

- A landlord who is tired of the meagre profits they are making from rental property

- A home-owner who wants to get extra income from their bedroom using Airbnb

- A property developer who is looking for creative ways to increase their cash flow.

You might be asking: what type of locations should the property be? I believe that serviced accommodation can be done anywhere in the world. This is because there is always demand for short stay accommodation anywhere you go. As an investor, the number one priority is to carry out your due diligence to find out the demand for your area. The following pointers might help you to make a decision: good infrastructure, easy access to transport, proximity to town centres, and existing serviced apartments in the area. You could research on websites like Airbnb if there are other people in your area and what kind of properties they have.

This will give you an idea of the demand for short term accommodation in that area.

What are serviced apartments ideal for?

This question is for an investor who is wondering which kind of people would be interested in living in serviced apartments. These include various types of people such as: professionals such as the police, teachers, nurses and doctors coming to work in an area for a few days. Then corporate clients like management consultants, engineers, construction workers and business travellers. Finally, regular tourists and leisure travellers. Let us now take a look at each of these groups.

Professionals

These are people working away from both their workplace and home. They usually prefer short to medium term accommodation. For those relocating to the UK, it's a lot of hassle to just come in and get permanent accommodation as the letting agents need a reference, and credit checks on the company or person intending to take on the property. If you are new to the UK, your credit check might not be successful because you are required to have stayed in the UK for at least 6 months.

The Individuals relocating to the UK or from elsewhere within the country may decide to try and settle in an area they like before they buy a property and learn about the housing market. They may wish for the flexibility of a short-term let to allow them to continue searching for a home to buy.

Corporate clients

The majority of short-term let clients come from the corporate world and they may be looking for short to medium-term accommodation for their staff. They might be coming to the area for training or relocating between offices. Serviced apartments makes the transition more comfortableand corporate guests will choose serviced apartments over traditional resorts and hotels. In addition, corporate guests include employees and managers attending conferences, exhibitions and trade shows. This group can also include sportsmen and sportswomen and their audience when major sports events are held such as annual events including Wimbledon or any major local events including sports events.

In addition, local councils and insurance companies often put people in hotels and serviced apartments while their homes are being repaired or while sorting out a family problem. However, if a family is likely to be kept away from their home for an indeterminate amount of time, the insurance company may consider it less traumatic, and more financially agreable to rehouse them in a serviced accommodation.

Tourists

The United Kingdom is blessed with a wide variety of tourist attractions as it is home to the Queen, the Big Ben, Parliament, palaces, museums, historic castles as well as beaches. There are different kinds of restaurants, cafes, art galleries, stadiums and theatres. All of these attractions are within walking distance of serviced apartments. In addition, there are people celebrating important life events such as weddings, funerals, birthdays that might want to stay in the same apartments rather than be scattered on different floors in a hotel.

Why invest in serviced accommodation?

Have you ever wondered and asked the question: Why should I invest in service apartment buildings?' Here are the reasons to invest in service apartments.

Multiple streams of income

By investing in service apartments, you are able to create several streams of income simultaneously from a single investment. There is no other investment option that I know of that can provide this kind of benefit without extreme risk to go along with it. If you looked at the financial statements from a serviced apartment, you will actually find 4 different streams of income simultaneously working together: Cash flow, appreciation overtime, principal reduction where your guest pay your mortgage balance, and tax benefits such as the ability to reinvest your profits without paying capital gains.

Having control

There are several forms of control that I like when investing in serviced apartments. Firstly, I have the ability to invest how I want. I can invest on my own, in a partnership, or in a group investment. I can choose the type of properties I will invest in and select their locations. Secondly, I have the flexibility to invest when I want. I am not not bound by any terms and conditions of a stock or mutual fund trading account. This means I choose when to buy and what to buy. Thirdly, you can invest and have someone else manage the day-to-day operations of a serviced apartment. Fourth and last, serviced apartments can increase in their value. This is probably the number one control reason I like. This is because with an apartment building, I can actually control the property value by affecting the net operating income of the property. In this way, I can easily add value to the property both in cash flow and future value.

Reliable cashflow for the landlord

As a landlord, when you rent out your serviced apartment, you enter into a long-term lease with a management company as opposed to an individual tenant. This method is commonly known as Rent to Rent. A management company will obtain the property from you and pay rental income as they provide short stay services to people. The management company then pays you the agreed rental rate for the term of the lease, usually with pre-negotiated rental reviews to ensure you're getting a good market rate. This makes serviced apartments a great option if you are looking for something that provides a reliable and regular cash flow. Effectively, long-term lease equals no voids for you as a landlord. The long-term nature of the lease with the management company means the usual concerns about loss of income when the property is vacant don't apply.

Maintenance

Owning a serviced apartment provides peace of mind knowing that the day to day maintenance is taken care of by the business operator. Daily room cleaning, minor repairs and any accidental damage are all covered under the lease and conducted without reference to the landlord who can rest easily knowing the apartment is looked after 24/7.

Major repairs or replacements of fixed appliances are the responsibility of the landlord, just as is the case in any other investment property.

32

CHAPTER 3

MODELS OF INVESTING IN SERVICED ACCOMMODATION

Rent to rent serviced accommodation

There are a number of risks in offering this type of rental accommodation and these will be highlighted later in the book. I also will share with you the key areas that need to be tackled to ensure that your serviced apartments stand out from the crowd and will bring in healthy rental profits.

Guaranteed rent is probably what most people think of when they hear of rent-to-rent serviced accommodation. It is very straightforward concept – you are guaranteeing monthly rent to a landlord, operating the property as serviced accommodation (obviously with their permission!), and making profit from the difference between your cost base and what you are able to charge guests on a nightly rate.

If we consider the model from a risk and reward perspective, the landlord is taking very little risk as they're going to get paid their money each month regardless of performance. At the same time they're getting a low reward, because they're only getting the same amount of money as if they were renting it out as a single let property. Conversely, as a serviced accommodation operator you are taking all of the risk and benefiting from all of the reward.

Landlord joint venture model

The concept of a Landlord joint venture (JV) is very simple. The landlord is going to have a set of costs for operating the property, as will you with things like cleaning, booking fees and maintenance. With a Landlord JV you split the profit after all of these costs, usually on a 50/50 basis.

There are two ways of considering the landlord costs. You can work on a true cost basis for the landlord, considering their mortgage, insurance, ground rent etc. Alternatively, you take the single let rent as their total cost, which is inclusive of all of their costs. The latter is certainly the more popular model, but typically a landlord would have to pay letting agent fees in order to let it out as a single let. It is not unfair to deduct a similar percentage to a letting agent – say 8-12% – from the amount which is considered as the landlords single let cost. Considered from a risk and reward perspective, you are sharing the risk and reward with the landlord. This might work particularly well if you are going into a new area rather than take on all of the risk yourself.

There are two other areas we should consider around this model that offer substantial benefits above the guaranteed rent model. First of all, when growing a serviced accommodation business there are likely to be two main things which will hold you back – getting enough deals through to continue to expand your business, and being able to fund them. One of the fantastic thing about this model is that they remove these growth barriers from your business. Because you are offering massive value to landlords, the potential to earn more money from their property rather than having to go out and chase deals, the deals will come to you.

People will start approaching you, and you will start generating referrals, because most landlords want to make more money from their properties. Finding deals is another area that holds many people back from growth, and this is negated by the Landlord JV model. There are no deposits to pay, no first month's rent up front and you agree with the landlord that they pay for the furniture and preparing the property for serviced accommodation. This is an easy sell, as in order to "unlock" the additional income of (for instance) £300-500 per month, they must first spend a few thousand to prepare the property. In terms of Return on Investment (ROI), this is probably the best money they will ever spend!

Even if you are well funded for your guaranteed rent deals, not having up-front costs still fundamentally changes the model. There is no an "earn back" period, or calculating loan repayments into costs – you are profitable from day one. In small business terms, a profitable business from day one is pretty much the holy grail!

The second area we should consider when comparing with guaranteed rent is VAT. With guaranteed rent, all of the guest's revenue will be in your name, meaning that after a couple of properties you will most likely hit the VAT threshold (and consequently lose a big chunk of your profits to HMRC!). With a Landlord JV, you structure the deal so that the income is in their name, and you are essentially acting as a management agent. In the same way that in residential property a letting agent deals with tenants and takes rent on behalf of the landlord, you will deal with guests and take payments on the landlords' behalf. Each month you invoice your share of the profit, which is the only money which contributes towards your turnover.

Sourcer joint venture model

The Sourcer JV works in exactly the same way as the Landlord JV, except you are working with a Sourcer rather than a Landlord. Generally, the Sourcer has agreed guaranteed rent with a landlord, and you are working with the Sourcer to run it as serviced accommodation while splitting the profit. This model can work really well for Sourcers, who rather than taking a one off fee for sourcing a property, can turn it into true "passive income", as they will not need to do any further work but will receive income from the property for the length of the deal.

Like the Landlord JV, they will need to put the initial cash in – but with good negotiation skills, this could just be the cost of the furniture (and there is always the option to rent). The issue with this model is mainly the scalability – as it is based on guaranteed rent, it comes up against the same issues that the guaranteed rent model does, as discussed above.

Management model

The Management Model is very different to the other models, as you get paid as a percentage of the turnover and not the profit. To reuse the previous analogy, you are acting as a "letting agent" for serviced accommodation in the truest sense. The money that you take in is on behalf of the landlord, the money that you pay out (for instance, cleaning or booking fees) is on behalf of the landlord, and each month they receive a settlement for you for the balance of income minus outgoings.

When we consider the risk and reward of this model, then you are taking very little risk. Should the property underperform and be losing the landlord money, you will still get paid your set percentage of the turnover. What really makes this model interesting is that it's the only model that can move away from the established "Risk and

Reward Line" – as although the risk is very low, the reward does not have to be. If you are charging around 20% for management, then typically your income is very similar to the Landlord JV model – but with much less risk.

A colleague from Southampton uses this model. She says that the reason that she has chosen the Management Model within her serviced accommodation business is because is scaling to a large level in a relatively short space of time. She has had a full time property manager from day one, is regularly adding new team members, and these staff need to get paid regardless of business performance. Seasonality is something she strongly feel is not talked about enough in serviced accommodation. Even in Southampton, which has a strong all year round market, it is typical to see a 20% drop in turnover for 3 months over winter. If your income is based on the profit of the deal – as with all of the other models – a 20% drop in turnover is going to significantly impact on your income.

With the Management Model, your income is based on turnover not profit – so if the turnover drops by 20%, your income drops by 20%. When you have significant overheads such as staff costs and offices, ensuring a regular and stable. There are many opportunities for rent-to-rent. These can be house of multiple occupancy or HMOs, below market value, buy-to-let, and of course, serviced accommodation.

Questions for new investors

Which type of apartment is the best?

If you are an apartment buyer and want to become a successful income investor, the best types of apartments to invest in are the smaller ones such as studios and 1 bed flats. The obvious reason is that smaller apartments are easier to rent than larger ones. As an owner, it is much more difficult to find tenants for a large apartment with many rooms. Naturally, you need to look for a family or a group of individuals who want to live together or you have multi-tenancies who prefer home-sharing.

All these simply mean all your other occupiers are taken out since they cannot afford either the 50% deposit or the fact that no bank would give what they need. Most of the owners of smaller apartments are investors which is perhaps the reason why they are categorized as investor apartments.

How do you measure the value of your apartment?

With the many sales methods used these days, it can be a really challenging task to find the true value of the apartment you're looking to invest in. The most effective way to accomplish this is through an apartment valuation tool which uses real world sales data and assess the property based on its current condition along with other important factors such as location, size, number of bedrooms, accessibility, amenities, general atmosphere, as well as the distance from the city and landmarks.

Having enough money is not everything to becoming a successful investor. You also need to be an educated and a well-informed buyer. To become such, you need to do research and check out reputable websites that offer various tools, guides, and updates on how to buy and sell apartments.

How do I work with a real estate agent?

When you find the right real estate agent to assist you in obtaining your apartment, you no longer have to do it all alone. This is a great option for the new investors. Most real estate agents know the ins and outs of the market. They will do a much better job in finding you the perfect home than you could do by yourself.

Another great advantage of hiring a real estate agent is their knowledge of all the homes available in a variety of neighborhoods. What information they do not already posses, they can easily obtain. They are able to access all the information on any home for sale within and the surrounding areas. They can easily tell you about the school system, crime rates, demographics, and much more. Having timely accessibility to this information will make choosing your home much easier.

A professional estate agent is going to also be able to advise you on the prices of these apartments. They can give you all the financial information you need to know about an apartment. They are also trained to help you weigh all the financial factors and create a blueprint of how you need to go about negotiating with the seller, and possibly their real estate agent, on the price.

A real estate agent is going to be able to save you a great deal of money on your apartment's purchase price. They can also negotiate any improvements you may want done prior to buying your apartment. Then there is the mountain of paperwork involved in purchasing a apartment. Your real estate agent is an expert on all the paperwork you will need to do in order to purchase an apartment. This is probably the best reason to work with a professional agent. Having a professional at your side will make your dream of going into service apartment business easier.

How to reduce risks when investing

The problem is that you can lose a LOT of money using real estate if you do it the wrong way. Let's look at a few ways to eliminate risk when using property investments to increase your cash flow.

Get an experienced mentor

Those who are most successful in using property investing for increasing personal cashflow have learned what they know from someone else. Very few people who are successful in using real estate for increasing cash flow got that way by the school of hard knocks. This is because a "trial and error" education in property investments can cost thousands and thousands of money in what Dave Ramsey calls "stupid tax." So, it's crucial that you get a mentor who is trustworthy and competent enough to coach you in learning about investing in serviced apartments.

Know your financial position

Before using real estate investing for increasing personal cash flow or personal wealth building, it's important that you have things together on the home front as well. This means that your personal finances in order, your expenses are less than 70 % of your net pay and that you have enough emergency cash in reserves to cover your expenses for three months.

It's also good to have a consistent habit of setting aside the FIRST 10% of your income for investing. This will empower you to focus on your investments to increase your cashflow without having to worry about whether you are about to invest the mortgage money. Even if you decide not to have these things in place, get a clear and WRITTEN snapshot of your financial situation before you start making a move towards real estate investing for increasing your cash flow or wealth building.

There is a process as you pursue that 'One big Life' that you deserve. I have a few ideas quickly summarised but you could always tailor it accordingly.

- Analyse your current situation
- Create an investment plan
- Attend trainings and workshops to leverage the experience, expertise and insights of people who have been there and done it.
- Network with others in the field by attending business or network meetings in your area.
- Start small or joint venture with other experienced investors. Would you like to be added to the JV email list? Email me at peaceproperty@yahoo.co.uk

The costs before buying property

Buy to let is arguably one of the most popular strategies of investing in property especially if you're just starting out to invest in property. Investors are making money by buying single family houses and letting them out for a small monthly rent or turning them into serviced apartments where guests pay on a nightly basis. They come either furnished or unfurnished and the landlord can give them to a management company to manage them on their behalf or they can be completely managed by the landlord.

To avoid any nasty surprises, here are a few tips to consider when buying in England.

- For legal issues, get help from your solicitors, licenced conveyancers and mortgage brokers

- If the property is worth over £125, 000, you will pay stamp duty ranging from 1% -7% of the property value.

- Some lenders may specify that you must have at least landlord buildings insurance in place.

- You need funds for decorating the property, and generally getting it ready for business.

- You need to have a registered electrician and a gas safety registered engineer to check if all the fixed installations and appliances are safe.

- You will also have to provide and display an Energy Performance Certificate in the property.

The Residential Landlords Association shows that the number of buy-to-let investors renting on Airbnb has seen a 54% increase between February 2016 and March 2017. This may be because short-term lets yield a higher rent.

Current data from Zoopla reveals that the average one-bed flat in London is let for £1,618 a month while a single private room on Airbnb could make an estimated £1632 per month. Increasingly, landlords are finding that Airbnb and other similar platforms are more lucrative than the standard longer tenancies model. The investor has to keep multiple factors in mind while purchasing corporate serviced apartments. Usually, such apartments offer strong returns at low risk as they are let on longterm.

CHAPTER 4

SERVICED ACCOMMODATION AND RENT TO RENT

Rent to rent strategy

So far we have looked at what serviced accommodation is and the opportunities it offers to landlords, management companies, and guests. In this chapter, we turn to the rent to rent strategy that is used by some management companies that run serviced apartments.

Rent to rent is very common in the United Kingdom and getting quickly recognised all over the world. It is where the landlord gets into an agreement with a property management company that they will pay the landlord a guaranteed rent for each month. In this strategy, any property in good order could fit perfectly for the serviced accommodation business. For example, multi-let/HMO (house of multiple occupancy) properties are used. If an HMO had 4 rooms, rooms can be let out individually or as a whole house to gets. You or the landlord needs to secure a licence from the local council known as the HMO LICENCE which allows more than 4 or more unrelated people to dwell in one property and share the basic facilities. Any type of property such as studios, one bedroom or two bedroom apartments can be used as a serviced apartment. We have had the properties in different categories and it all boils down to your financial goals.

Benefits of rent to rent strategy as a business

- It requires little money to start
- Generate income from a property you don't own
- Rooms in an HMO can be rented out on a nightly fee and obtain higher profits.

- Bills and utilities are all paid by the management company.

Local Authority requirements before issuing HMO licences

- Fire doors with fire resistant paint on doors and walls
- Smoke detection alarms
- Heat detection alarms
- Fire safety equipment like fire blankets, fire extinguisher, and general fire action procedure message on wall
- Room sizes
- Fire risk assessment.

Legal obligations

- Displayed Gas Safety certificate
- Periodic Electrical Testing (PET)

Get the right contracts

You have several types of contract and must use each individual contract in the right context.

If getting the property directly from landlord, you need a management contract similar to the one a letting agent would have with a landlord as you are operating on the landlords' behalf.

If you are getting the property from agent, you will need a common law tenancy (CLT) or Company Let (CL) - While the CLT is the best contract we can go for, most agents will run a mile if you pitch them a CLT. REMEMBER that the key point within the Common Law is that we need to make 2 changes. First, most contracts will state we cannot sublet, but that's EXACTLY our business model, so this clause will need removing. Second, most contracts will say we can place our EMPLOYEES within the property, but we need to change this to CLIENTS so it is fit for purpose. If they don't accept these changes, we cannot move forward.

If you are making a contract with the client/guest, you will need Terms & Conditions (T&Cs). The T&C's will dictate the rules and regulations by which guests should abide by while in your apartment. CLEAR T&C's are very important. Let us now turn to how to find your ideal property.

Finding good property deals

Knowing what makes a great property deal and how to find them, is the most important skill you should master if you want to be a successful property investor.

When you become good at finding deals, you will find more than you can possibly do yourself. You get to keep the best deals and the ones you don't want, you should package up and sell to other investors. This can be a very lucrative extra income stream for you.

First and foremost, do some market research and work out the leve of demand in your area. One way is to go to your local hotels in your area like Premier Inn, Hilton, Holiday Inn hotels and pretend you have a wedding coming up and you need to book out quite a few rooms. You then ask to view some of the rooms. While you are viewing, that's when you do your research. Ask them the following questions:

- How many rooms do you have?

- How busy are you on weekends and weekdays?

- Who normally stays here?

- How far do I need to book in advance? (this shows how busy they are)

- What is your rate on weekdays and weekends?

Once you have all this info from a few hotels, you should be able to work out the general demand in the area, which type of guests are booking (business or tourists) and get a better indication of price points. Using that data you can make better decisions when picking your area for serviced apartments. We did this in an area once and found out the hotel had a lot of guests who were staying with them for months as they were working in the local area and that another hotel was going to open up the following year.

Also, find out if it's a busy area where you want to start doing business, find out if theres an Airport, hospital, big shopping mall, near the motorway, is it near a university? In this kind of areas there are always people looking for short term accommodation you therefore start on the right foot in your serviced accommodation business. Usually these sort of places have a very good established transport system like trains, buses are all easy to catch.

Ways to acquire property to start business

Your home

You could start by rent out your house, flat or sparc room on Airbnb. The rent-a-room scheme also means the first £7,500 earned from letting out a furnished room, guesthouse, or bed and breakfast is tax free. This tax break also applies to short-term lettings such as those on Airbnb.

Airbnb has a secure payment system means you never have to deal with money directly. Guests are charged before arrival, and you are paid after they check in. If your guests get hurt, Airbnb protects you from liability claims up to a million dollars, included free for every Airbnb host.

Banner Ads

Place some banners in the high street over the weekend with your details and a contact on. We use a lead capture system that means we can keep marketing to the landlord once they have visited our website.

Letting agents and property developers

Develop good relationships with letting agents and property developers for new built apartments. Most landlords prefer to bring their properties to agents to manage everything right from finding a tenant to the management at a small fee. We got our first property from a letting agent who up to this day finds us good properties to do our business. Likewise, you can find very nice properties from them if you introduce yourself to them and tell them what you are looking for and they will be happy to help. I remember for us to get our very first property, it was difficulty as the letting agents were not willing to cooperate with us. We sought help from an expert who held our hand in the whole process of talking to different agents. At the end of the day, I was driving back home and one agent called me and asked if we were interested in a 4 bedroom house in town. This was a breakthrough moment for us.

Closing deals with the letting agent is actually one of the easiest things to do if you know how. Try keeping these key rules in mind. Back up your verbal proposal in writing. Make sure that anything agreed or spoken is clarified in writing. This keeps a paper trail and transparency in everything we do. The last thing you want is a dispute about the contract terms, rent, maintenance or anything else for that matter. Be clear, write it down and make them confirm they understand.

Be transparent. NEVER swerve difficult questions. Sub-letting is a classic. Always agree and let them know you will be operating under the legal framework. Know how to overcome the common objections: ONE OBJECTION

AT A TIME. Know your pitch and product. This seems obvious but know it inside out. Communicate it clearly and you will close more deals. Practice your pitch until it is watertight. Keep eye contact. If you are being honest and transparent this should be easy. Eye contact breeds certainty and reassurance.

Directly from the landlord

It is advisable to drive around the locations you intend to do business in. This will tell you the kind of neighbourhood and you could potentially be looking for a house that looks vacant, and using online public records to tracks down the owner of the property. Send the owner of the house an email stating your interest in using their property.

Look for landlords who belong to an accreditation scheme like the Residential Landlords Association who run national schemes. Call the landlords or send a first class stamp letter especially those who are listing properties "for rent" on Zoopla or Rightmove. You can easily find the details of the landlords by buying a public record list using sites like: The Gazette (the UK's official public record) and the HM Land Registry on www.gov.uk where you can download title deeds. Let the landlord know you are interested in renting, and the added value they will get when they rent the property to you. For example that, they will get guaranteed monthly rent, they will save on management fees.

What will landlords be looking for when you approach them?

Before you start to look out for landlords make sure you have the following in place. You need a clear plan on how long you want the property. Ask for a tenancy to be any time between 6 months and 7 years long. Think about how much rent you can afford plus the deposit needed to pay as initial costs. Have your documents ready. Landlords and agents will want to confirm your identity, immigration status, credit history and possibly employment status. Do you have the right to rent property in the UK? Landlords must check that all people living in their property have the right to rent must be aged 21 and above years. They will need to make copies of your documents and return your original documents to you. You may need a rent guarantor.

Serviced Accommodation Checklist

> ➤ Get an accountant when starting out as they will save you money by providing professional advice. They can help you with Setting-up the payroll if you

have some people you have employed and deal with the HMRC, VAT and tax liabilities.

➤ Decide if you are going to operate as a sole trader or as a limited company. If you choose a limited company, your accountant can help you register the company or do it yourself online

➤ Open up a business bank account.

➤ Deal with insurances such as Professional Indemnity and Public Liability to protect you against risks

➤ Register with the Data Protection Office (ICO) to show you are handling data correctly.

➤ Register with HMRC for Anti-Money Laundering

➤ Register with the Property Ombudsman Scheme to protect yourself and your clients

➤ Work on your brand - logos, website(s), and marketing strategy.

➤ Choose your Booking Systems and Online Travel Agencies (OTA's). These are platforms that will allow you to market your property to the world for a commission ranging from 3-17% of the value of the booking. They include: Airbnb, Booking.com, Laterooms, Lastminute.com, Tripadvisor, etc.

➤ Consider a Channel Manager such as Eviivo, Kigo, Tokeet which are platforms that will allow you to manage multiple properties across multiple booking sites. A MUST have if you're looking to scale.

CHAPTER 5

MANAGING SERVICED ACCOMMODATION

This chapter focuses on how to manage a serviced accommodation business. We will explore how to furnish your apartment and how to manage it on a daily basis.

Furnishing the apartments

People who choose to stay in service apartments do so for a reason. They don't want a hotel! So, give them the comforts of home. Invest in some decent quality goods.

- Decoration: Are you going to have a theme across all of your properties? A little of painting may be necessary but ideally you can do this with furnishings. Look for packages that match your style.
- Furniture, appliances, staging and soft fittings: If the property has come furnished you will want to do a complete check on all items for their suitability for use in the serviced apartment.
- Compliance with Fire Safety Regulations is paramount. You are therefore required to carry out a Portable Appliance Testing. This is commonly known as "PAT", "PAT Inspection" or as "PAT testing" in the United Kingdom, by which electrical appliances are routinely checked for safety.

- Check the mattresses are compliant
- Check bed frame is fire compliant
- Check wear and tear. Just because an apartment comes furnished, doesn't mean you shouldn't add or subtract furniture!
- Invest in good bedding and MATTRESS PROTECTORS!
- Get high speed Wi-Fi.
- SMART TV: Make sure your Wi-Fi works and People can use it for livestreaming.
- BLUETOOTH Radio: Doesn't need to be the latest tech. Simple but solid.
- Good professional photos for marketing. Take photos of the property inside and out, make the beds and set up the kitchen and house in order before taking photos so the house looks nice.
- Kettle, toaster, cups, plates etc. Non-stick pots and pans with wooden style utensils are always easier to clean. Always have tea, coffee, milk, sugar and, depending on length of stay, a small shopping hamper. Always have directions to the local supermarket. TIP: Always leave some welcome chocolates or biscuits.

Once you have done all the furnishing, take professional photographs which will be uploaded on your website, social media and online booking platforms like Booking.com and Airbnb.

Management and organisation Team

A team involves lots of people working together in agreement in order to meet the needs of guests and keep the business moving forward. In a serviced accommodation business, a team can consist of: an accountant, reception staff who usually meet, greet checkin and checkout guests, housekeeping staff, manager, and the public relations offer who deals with marketing and promoting the business online and locally.

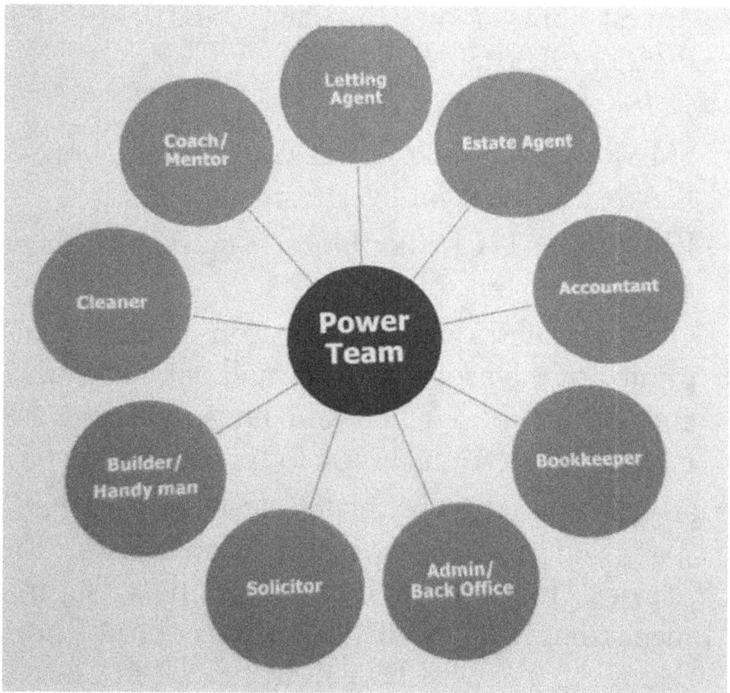

All staff require excellent customer service skills, attention to detail, team work, creative problem-solving skills (because guests like travelers sometimes have unexpected problems) and a thorough knowledge of local resources and attractions is important as well. Here is a brief overview of some of reception staff.

The reception or front-desk team meets guests at the property during the checkin hours usually from 2pm to 11pm. They are the first point of contact as guests need someone to show them around and also attend to any questions. These may involve extending their stay, expressing complaints related to the available amenities such as using the heating system, checkout and cancellation procedures, kitchenware, linen, etc. If you don't have the reception staff, you can use a key collection service. This is where the guest collects the key from a place like a pub, petrol station, corner shop or trusted team member or neighbour. Alternatively, you can have a Masterlock box mounted at the front wall entrance and guests are given a code when they arrive to get their key. It is advisable to have your work mobile phone pined in and outside the apartment so that guests can contact you directly.

Operations of a serviced apartment business

There are various operations that serviced apartment providers engage in. They include: checking in and checking out guests, managing reservations and enquiries, paying bills, communicating with guests and dealing with their complaints, and shopping for sundries. In the rest of this chapter, I am going to go through what these operations involve before, during and after staying.

Before staying

Checking in guests is one of the most important procedures you have to ensure a safe and positive experience. Remember the first impressions are everything. For efficient checking in, there needs to be communication with the guest prior to arrival. This should really be automated for best results. Emails, SMS texts and phonecalls can be made to guests to let them know what to bring when they come. For example, the guest will often need their passport or identity document, the credit or debit card they used to book and their booking confirmation. I normally call my guests before they arrive as it is a nice way of identifying any changes in their plans, or highlighting potential issues and opportunities. For example, in calling my guests, I have become aware of opportunities such as a big football match going to happen. This is why I am in favour of personal check-ins and good pre-arrival communication, this is where the meet and greet staff or front desk come in.

Also, contacting the guest before they arrive allows us to vet guests. You might also get guests who are abusive or under the influence of alcohol and drugs. Oftenly, these guests are from the same area where your apartment is and their personal details do not matching on booking portals. You also need to take into consideration the age of the guests. I wouldn't let in a group of four 18 year olds stay in my apartment. It is essential that you have a policy on how you decide whom you let into your apartment and let the guest know your hospitality rules. You can have this policy sent to the guests who book or put in on your website. In addition, have a checkin form where guest put their details, read the hospitality rules, and sign them before hand getting the keys.

Whether it is 4 builders or a sharply dressed business woman in her 50's… ALWAYS explain clearly the ground rules and consequences if these are breached. No smoking, no partying, no anti-social behaviour, etc.

During stay

Not that your guest has checked in, you need to follow up to see how their stay is going. Follow up every 24 hours to see if the guest is okay in the property. Do this via phone call. It's a great opportunity to ask for their email too if they didn't fill in the form before. So you can add it to your mailing list. This will allow you to contact them in the future so that they can book directly with you thus NO BOOKING FEES! Factor in regular email and text follow ups and the odd call throughout their stay. If the guests are staying for weeks or months do this periodically. As you talk the guests, you will identify some issues some of which might require your immediate attention.

You will be dealing with emergencies. For example, leaking pipes, power outages, lost keys and therefore no access to the apartment. It is important that you have a guest booked that explains what emergencies are and are not. It's best to have an operations manual or guest booklet for the apartment. This should explain how to use the oven, heating system, turn on the TV connect to the Wi-Fi and what to do if it cuts out. There have been times guest have called in the middle of the night saying that the Wi-Fi is not stable and to them, this is an emergency that needs immediate attention even when it might be outside your control.

Another issue worth mentioning is health and safety. **You need to c**learly indicate the fire escape routes, fire safety equipment and alarms in your apartment. Unfortunately we live in a world where some people are just downright nasty. Have a policy in place for how your staff should be treated. Go out of your way to show how you will protect them.

After staying

Once the guests have stayed, it is important that they get a smooth checkout. This might involve you arranging in advance someone to collect keys from them or letting the guest know how they will leave the apartment once they have stayed. As you would have included what to do when a key gets lost, make sure you charge the guests for any lost keys etc as per your T&C's. If they have taken them by accident give them a few days to return them by post. But be clear you WILL have to charge them.

As part of the checkout procedure, make sure you inspect the property for damages. Always have photographic evidence of any damages caused by the guest. This should be matched against your pre-checks of the property as proof the damage was caused by the guest. Make the guest aware of the damage and that you will be charging them accordingly. If you haven't performed the checks or the photos, don't bother. You won't legally have a leg to stand on. Always be nice when approaching these disputes via email. Have a written log of all communication and refer to the T&C's. Be reasonable in your charging.

Once the guest has left, you would want the apartment turned around as quickly as possible. So, have the apartment cleaned as soon as possible for the next guest.

DO NOT leave this till the last minute. It might be worth setting a WhatsApp Group to allow effective communication with your team. Little things like lightbulb not working or stains on the carpet can greatly affect the guest's experience. Give yourself as much time as possible to get these sorted. REMEMBER to have a procedure if there is an issue as it could impact the next guest.

Have all checks as part of a check-out procedure of which you or a member of staff can fill in and report back to you. Any significant issues will have to be dealt with immediately. Broken beds, boiler issues, or any significant damage can mean delays or even cancelled check-ins. Be honest and open and try to fix these issues as soon as possible. Then you can process these for maintenance if needed. Hook up with other SA providers and hotels locally to provide alternative accommodation. This is a great way to pass referrals and have them passed to you.

Cleaning team

Cleaning can be the HARDEST part of your business. If you find a good cleaner who is reliable HANG ON TO THEM! Treat them well as they are your eyes and ears. You must provide cleaners whether sole traders or commercial, with a CLEAR standard procedure. Try to create a checklist if not email me and I will get it for you. It It is likely that you will choose to have a linen supplier rather than purchasing linen yourself that you will then need to clean yourself. This would be costly and time consuming.

Linen suppliers offer the benefits of a drop off and collection service of clean/dirty linen items at reasonable costs. Sometimes when you only have 1 or 2 apartments it can seem quite steep on price. Fresh clean bedsheets are the starting point for a good night's sleep. This can set the tone for how your guests feel when they tell their friends, family and colleagues about their stay.

Periodic expenses

These include monthly or weekly expenses for your business. As you run your serviced accommodation business, you will need to pay bills such as electricity, gas, council tax, water rates, TV license, broadband, online travel agents, channel manager, rent or mortgage, cleaning company, laundry expenses, and merchant account.

You will also spend money on general house supplies such as cleaning materials, tea, coffee, sugar, milk, sweets, kitchen towels, toiletries, washing up liquid, washing powder, and dishwasher tablets.

Managing reviews

Getting good reviews is KEY to establishing your property. Here are some ways to get good reviews:

- Ask the guest nicely leave a review. You could start by saying, 'Hey, did you like the chocolates? If so please leave us a review, it really means a lot to us'
- Incentivise the guests with free giveaways or a chance to win a voucher.
- Send guests a survey via email and ask them for a review at the bottom of your survey

- Use social isolation techniques that allow people to behave in a certain way. For instance, you could put this message in the guest booklet, 'Most of our clients leave us a 5 star review on X website' this plays to our most basic sense of wanting to belong.
- Praise the guests and they make a request by saying, 'You have been such a great guest. Would you mind leaving us a review?'

Reservations Management System

If you are going to have a website that takes bookings, you will need to integrate with a channel manager and payment gateway. An example would be Eviivo or Kigo or Tokeet. It's important to get training on how to understand channel managers and how they work as this will stop you getting double bookings. Also, you want to integrate a payment gateway like stripe so they can book directly.

When looking for a property management system for your serviced apartments, take into account the following:

- How will drive your direct bookings?
- What revenue distribution tools are available?
- How is it set up for multi-locations?
- What are the corporate profiling and options?
- Are other serviced apartment providers using them?

Having a management system which can connect your apartments to hundreds of channels such as Booking.com, Airbnb and Expedia with real-time, two-way integration allows guests to make direct reservations through their desktops and mobile devices. Managers and owners of serviced apartments will easily be capable of achieving front-office duties all done with this system in place, such as booking reservations, guest check-in/check-out, room assignment, managing room rates, and billing.

Payments

There are different payment methods that can easily be integrated with your channel manager. Accepted payment methods differ depending on the country. In England the most common ones are: Stripe, Worldpay, Firstdata, and Payzone. In some cases guests may request or you may request that a bank transfer is done and is successfully received by cash, credit or debit card. For your business to be hands free, you require a merchant account to enable you to take credit and debit card payments over the phone. You can also take cash if you have security with you and make sure to check it that it's not fake money. Make sure your merchant account can pre-authorise a damage deposit from the card as well. Trust me, this will save you an awful lot of time and hassle in the future.

And if you don't like the idea of having to speak to people over the phone, there are also merchant accounts that can integrate with invoicing systems so all you need to do is send the electronic invoice.

The challenges of running serviced apartments

Serviced apartments constantly faces all kind of challenges. Many of them are common and involve safety problems and issues with guests. On one occasion, I had a coaching call from the person wanted to start his service apartment business. I explained first of all that people always talk about the rewards but no one talks about the failures or the daily grind. You can do it and I will support you but it will be hard work and late nights so are you ready to commit? It's so worth it, the returns are good. My mentee didn't return back because of fear.

Learning curve

One of the challenges is the amount of learning you will need that is so important for your business. Things like, how to vet your guests (THE MOST IMPORTANT IN THE BUSINESS, IT CAN MAKE OR BREAK YOU). So, you can sieve out the Bad ones, The Gang, The Party People, The Trouble makers that damages and disrespect your property, or the ones that takes over your property like a Tenant I had to evict. Vetting guests allows you to take only genuine, responsible and repeatable ones.

Damages

I'd like to say that the majority of our guests are really awesome and normally don't cause any problems during their stays. However, in some cases I have had to deal with guests that caused damages and are ungrateful. I have had guests break furniture, water taps and damage the walls. Some break glasses and smoke inside the rooms although they are forewarned of a charge, you will find the smoke alarm covered with a sock and smelling smoke inside.

Bad reviews

There was one guest who gave me 2 rating for my property because it had no ironing board and a few other things like no TV. I guess he had a right to do it, but to be honest, it felt badly as the TV was not listed on my apartment. I also need to mention that I had almost all 5 ratings for this same apartment. Although I was extremely angry, I wanted to appear as a professional host for my other guests. I explained in the answer to that review that rules are rules for all. But I am sorry and as we grow we will add more exciting items for the best guest's experience. I have now tried to improve as much as possible by listening to the guests' needs and interests. We also makes sure to list exactly what will be offered at the property so that there are no surprises when guests arrive.

Cleaning up after a wild party

Sometimes the cleaning services had a really hard time getting the place in order with some especially messy guests. I remember this first time when our guests, who were a couple of students, had a wild party at the apartment and left an awful mess. The thing is that there were only 2 guests that I rented out the apartment to. But apparently, they invited some friends.Always take pictures if they find an apartment messed up and things damaged, in this case we can fine the guests who have done it. We also charge a cleaning fee to our guests upon booking with us.

If you only own one property and you still clean it yourself, you may only need professional services from time to time. But there's no way you can handle it with multiple properties. One important tip: Make sure that the cleaners also tackle those often overlooked tasks, such as cleaning the oven and fridge, dusting, remove cobwebs and emptying the dishwasher.

Demanding guests

Once a guest wanted to leave two hours after the checkout time. At first, I agreed to this without additional payment but he ended up leaving almost 6 hours after the time of check-out. Thank God, I did not have more guests on the way that day. Sometimes, people just keep demanding additional amenities or services like free airport pickups. We have certain rules that I expect our guests to follow. We made a welcome booklet which we leave inside the room on the table in every property. And ask our guests to go through it carefully. If you want your bookings to go smoothly, enforce your rules and establish good communication to avoid some major headaches.

Cash backs from online payments

This happened to us several times as people were using a trick. Someone checking in had a different name and the payment card had a different name. These sorts of people actually booked for a month paying lots of money and after their stay they would ask for their money back that someone stole their card details which would be refunded back especially if you have no evidence of their stay.

Theft

I recently heard of a story from one of the other service providers that a guest came in for one night and early in the morning took everything in the apartment. There is also problems with squatters. A squatter is a person who unlawfully occupies an uninhabited building or unused land. We experienced this first hand when a guest refused to pay and also refused to leave the apartment after he had stayed there for a while. When we called police, we were told it's a court case and so he kept staying there with no pay. He changed the locks of the apartment.

CHAPTER 6

INCREASING YOUR CASH FLOW

Increasing personal cash flow

Cash flow is the net amount of money that a business receives and disburses during a given period of time. For your serviced apartment business to stay a flot, you need to have positive cash flow. Increasing your cash flow through investing in property has always been a popular method for personal wealth building. Think about it, housing represents a consistent tangible need and as long as people are interested in it, it will remain one of the best strategies for increasing personal cash flow and building wealth. As an individual, here are some of the ways you can increase your cash flow.

Become a host

Listing your empty room in your home on Airbnb allows you to make money from your property by renting it out on a short-term basis. Stays often range from one night to a few months. People will pay you good money to stay in your spare room in your home or your entire home. It's a great way to earn quick money and host guests from all over the world. Not only do you get to pick and choose who stays in your home, but you are in essence running a business from the comfort of your own living room.

You can "wow" guests with extra services which can be designed to make their stay extra convenient, such as free or paid airport transfers or food being readily stocked up in the fridge upon arrival, or more luxurious offerings such as chauffeur service, or champagne and flowers in room. You could develop a line of your own branded products like shampoo, soaps, t-shirts, robes or linens to sell to guests.

If you have space in the same or other rooms, one of the best investments to boost your occupancy and nightly rate is to add extra beds. For example, a pull-out coach or folding bed would allow for two more guests, giving you more flexibility in terms of the number of guests your listing can accommodate.

Referral fees

In the event that you get a qualified guests that are looking for short stays but all of your units are full, then you can refer that guest out to another service provider like you in your area who may have an empty apartment that night for a small fee .

Property management

You can start managing property for other landlords in your area. You can earn up to 6 to 10% commission on monthly rent rolls that you bring in to the landlord. Not only can you make some extra money but you can also find out more info on what is going on in that neighborhood and make valuable networking contacts on potential upcoming property deals.

Deal sourcing

While you're working on your property management and have knowledge of upcoming deals, you can farm those out to other investors for a finder's fee. Sourcing a deal can bring you in a quick £300 to £1000 for finding a deal for an investor.

If you're really good with numbers and know an area well, occasionally you may be asked to come in and review a deal for another investor. They will often pay a fee ($£100$ and up) to have you review the deal and give your opinion. It is not uncommon for an investor to pay to a seasoned investor to review the property and walk through during an inspection and give thumbs up or thumbs down on the deal.

Short term rentals

Once you feel you've mastered your first property, scale up, the next step is to increase your rental income by adding on another property to your business. One more investment property added to your real estate investment portfolio can mean more positive cash flow and rental income.

Maximise your bookings

Wherever you live, people are looking for accommodation. It's time to sharpen your skills and cash in. Keeping your calendar up-to-date is one of the easiest ways to increase bookings. The obvious reason being that staying on top of your listing's availability ensures that all your open dates appear on the Online Travel Agents' websites like Airbnb (so you don't miss any potential bookings). In addition, Airbnb's algorithm tags hosts who regularly update their calendars as both active and responsive. Make sure you log into your account as often as possible. Active and responsive hosts are rewarded with priority seating in the search rankings (and generally attract more interest). This level of involvement would clearly involve high commitment on your end, refresh your calendar every day, so you can carry your listing up that one extra step.

Reviews (especially positive ones) help to increase sales on any Online Travel Agency website. Good reviews are the backbone of a bestselling listing and the frame of trust that comes along with a healthy reservoir of reviews can almost guarantee more bookings and higher search rankings.

You need to have a completed profile on any travel websites where you advertise your listings. This falls under Airbnb's reward system – the more active that you are, the more seriously you take the Airbnb process, the more you will show up at the top of search results. Make sure that you have completed with detail each and every section of your listing on Airbnb or any other online portal you are using to market your apartments. What you are doing here is demonstrating that you are worthy and responsible enough to host guests. And of course you are, so it is your job to work it.

You will also need to have a competitive price, easy and simple. Check what is offered in your neighbourhood and, if possible, beat the price of the similar listings that are your competition. Also use the extra charge per person option, have a lower price for 1 person then gradually increase for added guests. This will make your pricing fairer.

As you host regularly, you will grow a list that you can later use to marker to your guests directly. Gather contact information including the guest's email address. Social media networking sites can help keep you in contact with prior guests and engage with new potential clients. Develop relationships, create special offers for returning guests, and create an email newsletter to keep your name "front of mind". The best way to double your short term rental income is to set a target and have the right business plan aligned with your overall vision.

Hosting experiences

Julian

My husband and I were looking for a way to earn some extra income early 2015. Then, my husband came across Airbnb where we listed our spare room. It was scary at first as we didn't know what to expect but using Airbnb has been exciting and very profitable for us. We got to meet lots of people and some are like family to us now. A year later, we started running a serviced accommodation business.

We decided to get property education and business coaching. We attended various courses with Legacy Education, Progressive Property, Intelligent Property and Les Brown Institute. These courses included: lease options, buy to let, rent to rent, commercial conversion, houses of multiple occupation, raising finance, and serviced accommodation and personal development.

With these property education providers, we expanded our knowledge on how to invest safely in property, source properties, and raise funds creatively. Now we offer mentoring and coaching to anyone who is looking for extra income like we did.

Robert

My first experience as an Airbnb guest was early 2015. I booked a hotel room during a time when 3 major international events were being held in the city. The hotel had doubled booked my room and unfortunately I arrived last. Forgetting how stupid this hotel policy was and the fact that the only room available in the city was a $15000 a night presidential suite, Airbnb came to my rescue.

It was the closest thing to the city, near a light rail station but not much else and it was a two storey town house with way too many bedrooms for myself. Otherwise, it was possibly the most enlightening and pleasant thing I could have hoped for. The place was immaculate, the furniture comfortable, and the hosts were fantastic. They came to check in on me after I checked in and we had a good chat. The extra space and kitchen meant I could invite over a close friend for an impromptu dinner and it was secluded such that I had a much better sleep than I could get in the city I would hazard.

It was a little more expensive than I budgeted for but considering the circumstance… I always consider AirBnB nowadays when travelling alongside hotel accomodation.

I have also been a host for a while now and superhost for the last couple of months. I find 80% of the guests I host are great! Almost suprisingly so because the other 20% can be almost hard to deal with. Every time I check in a group of guests I cross my fingers.

I always try my best to accomodate their needs but sometimes expectations outweigh the possibilities. Often guests come expecting hotel-like service, which, of course, is impossible for a private residence. Some of the things that have crushed my faith in guests include:

A group of guests arrived several hours after their stated check in time, complained there was no airport transfer, called roughly 3 times daily for menial things for example asking us to bring them drinking water when there was a shop near from the place and they had been provided 10 gallons already. They ended up leaving a small mountain of open rubbish in the middle of the kitchen after the left. I was forced to clean beer, wine and food stains off the floor for hours afterward.

We have had another group of guests break the front door lock after losing the key and not telling us about it until they had left. At least they had bought a new lock for us to install… Had multiple guests confirm a check in time only to completely ignore it, turning up several hours late, generally with the explanation that they didn't realise i would literally be the one waiting for them, not some "servant" (people here find it wierd we don't have a maid and private driver). Installed a keyless entry system in response and have had several guests complaining that I was not there to check them in personally.

I had a guest book then call 2 hours before arriving threatening to cancel and contact Airbnb because there were 2 flights of stairs to reach the apartment and she was a bit older. Then arrived and promptly said she would stay the entire time she booked, then in the end blocked the plumbing.

Guests constantly leave the air conditioning and lights on 24/7 resulting in exhorbitant bills. Safe to say, Airbnb hosting is a sometimes rewarding, sometimes head scratching and sometimes revolting experience.

It has allowed my wife and I to generate income on a property that is probably more than renting it out normally, but factoring in the higher bill costs and the incredible amount of work we put into the property to make sure its absolutey spotless for each guest (professional cleaning and laundering) it is probably a 10% extra we make.

Andrew

One month after moving into a two-bedroom apartment above our budget, my New York City roommate and i explored ways to make some extra money. We had used Airbnb as travellers and wondered about becoming hosts.

I would build our online profile, creating a listing and fielding reservations, and Michael would handle the actual hosting in the East Village, welcoming guests and pointing them toward our favorite bodega. If we could lower our $2,525 rent by even $100 to $200 per month, we reasoned, our time would be well spent. Few people (us included) would rent their room, apartment or house out to strangers if not for such a reward. Since its inception in 2008, Airbnb has wanted that to be more than money—rather, community, where you treat travellers from near and far the way you would want to be treated on your own trips abroad.

Of course, hiccups do happen. Not having air conditioning or a sparkling-clean bathroom would end up costing us with some of our initial visitors. Over our first nine months, though, Michael and I turned the minor complaints and honest feedback of 42 guests into $9,655. We earned 30 (mostly positive) reviews from singles and couples occupying my relatively large bedroom when I was out of town or staying at my girlfriend's for the weekend. (We also lucked out because New York City only barred the renting of whole apartments, not single rooms.)

The numbers make it sound seamless, but we made more mistakes along the way. A Puerto Rican couple that had "the best vacation of our lives" was followed by a Chinese toddler drawing colorfully on our walls. A Pennsylvania couple getting enough rest in my bed before running the New York City Marathon gave way to Southern California college girls trying to scam us for a free stay. Hosting experience is choppy but it can also be rewarding, particularly if you shorten your learning curve by considering ours first.

These are great stories from people who have been in the service accommodation business. I believe these will encourage you to get started in the service accommodation business this year.

CHAPTER 7

PROPERTY INVESTMENT

Get the right guidance

Good planning is essential to your financial success. Seeking advice from established experts in the field means that you have access to their valuable experience and knowledge about what works and what doesn't.

Assembling a good team of property investment professionals ensures that you have the support you need through every step of the process. The first member of your support team should be a Qualified Property Investment Advisor (QPIA). They will know the right formula to follow to ensure your success and will help you apply that formula to your circumstances. Next, you will need an experienced mortgage broker, licensed buyer's agent and a solicitor/conveyancer.

You will also need an independent pest and building inspector and a reliable property manager but if you have found a good buyer's agent that focus on building a relationship rather than a transaction, they will be able to provide you with some recommendations for a reliable property manager. And finally, to complete your 'A-Team', you will need a good accountant.

When searching for a team of people that you can trust, always assume yourself in a General Manager position. After all, if you want to build a passive income for life, this is a serious business. Look to see that they have a track record of performance and success and ask for testimonials where necessary. Most property professionals also offer a free consultation so make full use of the time and prepare your own list of concerns.

During the consultation, listen and observe if the advisor is trying to push you to buy a certain type of property or they are keen to understand your situation first before advising you on anything? One of our pet hates are advisors that try to recommend a one-size-fits-all solution when the fact is, every household is different.

Each household should have a property investment strategy that is custom built and tailored to their specific needs. You would want to make sure that your concerns are addressed and that you feel a sense of rapport. Always remember that your team is working for you and you want to make sure you feel confident and comfortable with them from the beginning.

Increase your borrowing power

Taking all possible steps to improve your credit and increase the amount of money you can borrow will benefit you greatly. Although some might say you don't need much to start investing in property, a bit more capital never hurts. You can start by consolidating your existing credit debt and decreasing the number of credit lines you have open. As always, saving as much as possible through effective budgeting is an essential part of this process.

If you have reached the point where you own more than one property, your borrowing power is enhanced by the rental income. Plus, the more good assets you have, the more attractive you are to lenders. Don't worry, however, if you don't own multiple properties. Even if you don't own a single property yet, focus on making your first purchase and then go from there. You might be surprised at how the momentum can build.

Set specific goals

Putting together a plan to create your ideal property portfolio is a fundamental step. You will be much more likely to achieve your goals once they have been clearly laid out. This is where you will need to have a discussion with a property investment advisor to assess your current finances and examine where you want to go.

What kind of specific goals do you want to achieve, and when do you want to achieve them? You will be looking at projections for your future financial needs and using that information to help make decisions right now. It can be beneficial to put your goals into a timeline so that you can plan more effectively. This will also help you gauge your success over time and make changes as necessary. Life is always full of expectancy, so embrace it!

A good QPIA will be able to crunch the numbers for you, analyses and determine the best investment strategy for your circumstances and explain everything in a way that you can understand using graphs and charts. This is really helpful because you will be able to see all the aspects of your portfolio in one place and pinpoint specific times in the future where you would be expecting a negative cash flow and even times when you can get to leave your day job to reap the benefits of your investments. You might be surprised at how simple this information can be when you have had a professional effectively break it down and present it to you.

Do your research

Knowledge is empowering. In addition to having solid help from experienced property investment professionals, keeping up to date with market trends is important to make sure that you are able to make informed decisions. Read as much as you can about choosing the right property, the loan process, and real estate in your target area so that you will be an educated and savvy buyer. Although you'll have the advantage of professional help, the more knowledge you have on your own, the better prepared you'll be to navigate your investments over the long haul.

At the very least, when the advisor is explaining things such as capital growth, rental yield returns, mortgage protection insurance, loan to value ratios, positively geared property, negatively geared property and so on, you would have an idea on what is at stake and be able to validate his advice. Even having a basic understanding on tax law will be beneficial. Although tax information can be difficult to understand, a little basic knowledge goes a long way when it comes to staying informed. It will also help when you are making decisions to renovate or upgrade your investment property.

Inspect the property

It goes without saying that any type of asset you purchase should be well built so that it stands the test of time. When it comes to property investment in particular, that becomes even more important.

Purchasing property requires significant sums of money, so you want to make sure that your purchase will be as profitable as possible. A good property inspection can reveal safety issues that may make the property unsafe to rent without considerable investment upfront. For all you know, the property might need a complete re-stumping that was not obvious and wasn't mentioned by the selling agent. These kind of hidden issues can cause significant financial damage to your portfolio.

A good and independent pest and building inspector can also help you anticipate future maintenance costs so that you can factor that into your profit projection. Apart from the actual property, the legislative part of it needs to be thoroughly reviewed as well, preferably by an experienced solicitor or conveyancer. The contract of sale is generally created to favour the seller and what many investors fail to realise is that key areas in the contract are actually negotiable.

Inexperienced investors often make the mistake of skipping this step only to find out later that the contract is disadvantageous for them. There are times when important details are hidden between the legal jargon such as ownership titles and building permits. With professional help, you may also learn about legal issues that you would not have known about. Finding a surveyor and solicitor that you trust is of the utmost importance. Albeit, this means another couple of hundred pounds to spend but would not it be wiser to spend it now rather than potentially losing thousands in the future? You do not want what should have been an asset to turn into a liability because something was missed during the process.

Take action

Time is of the essence more than ever when it comes to buying real estate. Procrastination is probably your worst nightmare. So, making a list ensures you can organise your "plan of attack" and is useful for deciding what to do next.

Even if you only accomplish one item per day, you will be very close to realising your ultimate goal of financial freedom. It can feel overwhelming when you initially think about everything that is involved with property investment. If you can break it down into manageable action steps, you'll feel much more confident as you begin the process.

A good first step is to schedule a consultation with an investment professional. You will feel assured and confident about moving forward when you have solid help on board at the start. With the right guidance and information, you can make real estate investment a profitable part of your life and retirement plan. It is definitely one of the best ways to "work smarter not harder." Once you have started with property investment, you will build momentum that will push you towards financial freedom and independence.

CHAPTER 8

MORTGAGES FOR AN APARTMENT

Mortgages for an apartment

If you are thinking about buying an apartment, here are some of the questions you will be asked when arranging finance to purchase the property:

Location, Location, Location

City fringe and the suburbs are more attractive to lenders as there are fewer apartments outside the inner city. Within the city centre, there are a number of apartments. The potential for over-supply means banks are concerned that if they need to sell the apartment in the event of a default on the loan, they will not get a good price.

Size matters

The bigger the size the better. If there are multiple apartments in a complex, this is less attractive to the banks and the more there are, the less they like it. Number of bedrooms compared to the size of the apartment also counts. If two apartments that are the same size, one with three bedrooms will be less desirable than one with two. The banks determine how much money they are likely to make if they have to sell the property. So more bedrooms in a small apartments will mean the bedrooms are smaller and the property harder to sell.

Conversion or purpose-built?

Was the property specifically built as an apartment complex or was it converted from a previous type of building? There are conversions found in the UK because it is easier to convert say an office block into apartments, than building it from scratch. These will become a thing of the past as they are less likely to comply with new building standards. A house split into two is still considered a residential property.

Who is borrowing the money?

Banks will also do an individual assessment of the person borrowing the money. They will take into account the borrower's ability to repay or service the loan, the size of their deposit, and where the deposit is coming from (and whether they saved it themselves).

Construction quality?

Apartment lending criteria is still affected by the same issues in regard to the exterior cladding type. When purchasing an apartment, it is very important to check structure records from surveyor for any history of leaking issues.

Planning class for your serviced apartment?

Here is a simple summary from a planning consultant and investor from the local authority in England. Planning for serviced accommodation is a grey area. There is no specific use class covering serviced accommodation operating a single unit is VERY different from operating a block like a hotel. Then you will be classed as C1 and need planning permission for change of use. 'A certificate of lawful development for change of use from C3 to C1 will be required. This is because, C3 is long-term residential i.e. homes and flats whereas C1 is for leisure and short-term residential. This would cover you because you would have a certificate that covers you for C1 use'.

Inquire also about the planning permission especially planning in London area and how to deal with a 90 day rule. The best way to work within the London Regulations, would be to restrict your SA lettings to less than 90 nights and find a series of short stay guests/tenants for 91+ days – documenting tenancy agreements on file if asked and to prove compliance.

Types of mortgages

Commercial lenders have been lending on short-term propositions for decades; guesthouses, B&Bs, hotels, holiday lets, even kennels and catteries.

When it comes to mortgages, lenders tend to treat short-term lets differently from HMOs, for example, a lender's primary concern is serviceability of the mortgage payment. With any normal tenancy, this is pretty simple. You have five ASTs for your HMO so the lender can see the monthly income will be based on these ASTs and thus determine your ability to meet the mortgage payments. It's not so straight forward with short-term letting because the lender has no idea what your income from it will be. In their eyes, they have no idea what you will be earning month to month, you could be full one week, but empty the rest of the month.

Lenders being lenders will always look on the pessimistic side and if they can't see a guaranteed income, they will assume the worst and that means no mortgage because you cannot prove you can service the mortgage from the property income. So, how can you legitimately fund an apartment property? The solution has been applied to short term lets for decades and it is all about your occupancy rates. For an established short-term letting business, you will be able to show the lender your historical occupancy rates.

They usually want the previous 12 months to base their lending on i.e. if you were at 86% occupancy for the previous year the lender will assume you will do a similar percentage in the coming 12 months and lend on the basis of that level of income. However, a lot of investors are coming into this new and don't have a track record, or are buying a new property to operate on an service apartment basis. At first glance you would fall at the historical occupancy fence, but there could be ways to still obtain borrowing.

If you have been running a service apartment business for at least 12 months, then are now adding to your portfolio, whilst you cannot show historical occupancy for the property you are about to buy, you can show it for your business as a whole. Some lenders will use the percentage you are already achieving and project that onto your new property, so you can borrow at that projected income level for your new property.

If you are brand new to serviced apartments, it becomes more challenging as you don't have any track record to offer a lender. There are two possible ways to overcome this. First, joint venture with an existing service apartment provider or experienced landlord, either buying in joint personal names or as joint shareholders in a limited company. After a period you can establish your own occupancy rates and no longer need the other person for future purchases.

CHAPTER 9

WHAT IS STOPPING YOU

What is stopping you from starting your business?

You have been thinking about starting your own business but you just cannot take the first step? It may be because you do not know or maybe you are afraid of something. It could be a little of both, fear and not knowing what to do. Just concentrate on putting a plan in motion and take it one step at a time. Here is some friendly advice that might help you along the way.

Be prepared for rejection

You will hear a lot of NOs during your starting phase. You are new and not many people know your brand yet and it's possible there several serviced apartments right down the street to yours. DO NOT, I repeat DO NOT let this discourage you. Acknowledge it, step up, and continue.

If you fall, get right back up

There will be times where you will feel like the whole world is against you. Where you cannot make a sale for the life of you but at this point it is KEY to continue plowing through. It only takes one small break to make it big. If you stop when you fall, you are limiting yourself to finding out what really is ahead or what your true potential is.

If someone is already doing it, do it better

Just because there is a serviced apartment down the street does not mean you cannot start your own successful business; just do it better! Offer something better, you have greatness inside you.

Just do it!

Yes, Nike shoes said it first but it applies to all! What is keeping you from just doing it? Fear? Fear is not our own worst enemy. No, let me clarify it; WE are our own worst enemy. We allow fear to take over and paralyze us to a point of no return. We sabotage our own beliefs and start thinking that we just can't do it. Then we stop. Put those thoughts out of your mind and focus on just doing it! Some of the wealthiest men and women out there live by this rule and so should you! Now, what's stopping you?

Our imagination is endless if we know how to use it.

With a positive attitude, determination and belief, you can create anything you imagine. And profit from it. Working for someone else might make you a living, but it won't make you rich. You need to think outside the square. And the direction that will set you on your way to success is with technology.

Everyone uses some form of technology everyday. And with some good creative thinking and imagination you can profit from all that is readily available at our fingertips. Property business is creating thousands of new entrepreneurs of all ages. Your never too young or too old. If you can think it, you can do it. It's that simple.

Imagination is endless. You just need to learn to use it. What are your ideas and dreams for the future? Write them down. Every success story started with an idea and the imagination to make it happen. Every rich and successful person in the world today started the same way.

CHAPTER 10

SECRETS TO SUCCEED

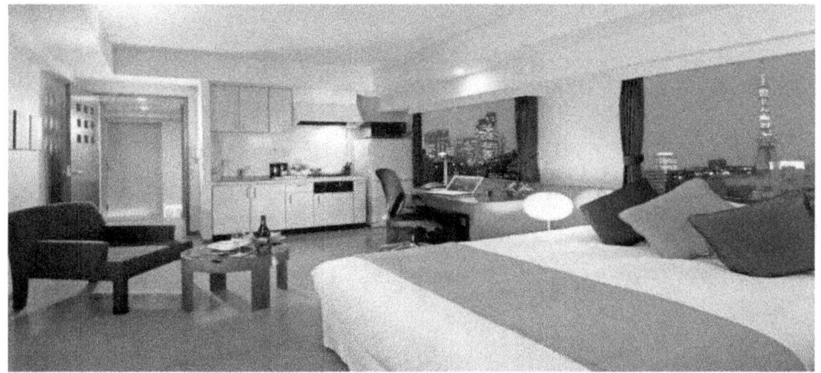

Many investors have thought about serviced apartment buildings but just do not know where to start. They have perceived barriers in their way and simply never get started. This is a shame because apartments are one of the most profitable businesses you can invest in and one where you can start with very little, and grow your wealth fast. Here are the secrets to success when investing in service apartments.

Always be learning

All the successful investors I know of are constantly learning. They are also voracious readers and read several books per month. This commonality is not at all surprising because it is a trait found in successful people in all areas of business. If you are serious about getting started in investing in apartments and becoming successful, you will need to educate yourself on this type of business. You could sign up for and read the industry trade magazines. You could attend seminars and trade shows that you find interesting. You could continue reading books not only on real estate, but other business, finance, and personal success.

Stay focused on your goals

If you ask anyone that has become successful in the serviced apartment business, they will tell you that a big part of their success is having goals and staying focused on achieving them. Yes, you have probably heard this about 1,000 times before, but there is a key difference here. It is not about just having a big dream, or a big goal. It is about having focused intent with a lot of emotion on your goals. Find that nagging, driving, gut-wrenching reason inside you, and nothing will stop you. You will simply enjoy what you are doing. That is the difference between those that simply have a vague goal and those that continue to drive toward success in the face of adversity. Finding your reason is key to your success.

To get what you want out of life, you must take massive action. To become successful in the service apartment business, you cannot stop after looking at a few properties, or taking a weekend seminar. You must take action and get that first property. Once you have that property, work to maximize its returns and value. Then repeat the process over and over.

I remember when I and my husband started attending property seminars, we learnt a lot and we were fired up and ready but the actual looking for the properties was not easy. It involved making phone calls to estate agents, landlords, visiting the properties to discern if they are suitable, it took a while until we actually got a mentor who helped us on our journey. Within no time and with the mentor, we started acquiring the properties and setting up for business. I would like you to know that starting small is a good place to start. Dream big, start small, and work your way toward larger and larger projects. The excitement is truly in the journey toward building your business.

Power to achieve anything in business

People fail because they don't realise how long it takes to succeed. Most people hunt for microwave deals. When you are building a property business, or any business for that matter, the biggest obstacle to overcome is your own discouragement and fear.

That small voice in your head that whispers:

- "You're not good enough..."
- "You're not smart enough..."
- "You're not experienced enough..."
- "You're not worthy of success yet..."

It's easy to end up in a rut, side-tracked by a private conversation going on in your head.

To overcome this voice, you need three things. First, have a proven process you can follow. When you're following a process, you don't get discouraged so easily. Every setback you experience just becomes feedback on the road to success. Second, get a group of people who will hold you accountable, but also help celebrate your progress. Third, get the right knowledge. You can't solve a problem with the same information you already have. Improving your knowledge of serviced accommodation is one of the fastest ways to increase your property income. There isn't another property strategy that can provide the same results from so little capital. You don't need big resources to get started. It's worth knowing that the serviced accommodation market is forecast to double in the next two years. Wherever you live, I there are golden serviced accommodation opportunities in your local area.

CONCLUSION

An investment in knowledge pays the best interest," Benjamin Franklin pronounced grandly in one of his 275 most famous proverbs. Serviced accommodation continues to grow in demand in the hospitality industry, so it's an exciting time to investigate making money in such an innovative way. Put in your due diligence, define whether the serviced accommodation business is for you, and then, if it is, take the plunge! If you liked this book, I would really appreciate it if you would leave a nice review. This will immensely help our future readers. So, what is your next step? Read on the next page and see if I might be able to help you.

1-2-1 Mentoring

You can leverage the wisdom and strategies that Julian Businge and her husband have used to build a large brand in serviced accommodation while staying true to their personal mission of being of value and service to global communities. Connect and learn if you are:

- Looking for help starting your serviced accommodation business
- Looking for help systemising and scaling your serviced accommodation business
- Looking for one-to-one assistance with Serviced Accommodation

Julian Businge offers a unique service to ensure you get your first property up and running smoothly. You will have access to her personal power team and a tailor-made work plan to kick start your business.

Once you've found your first deal, Julian will help you through the setup process. You will get access to our supplier lists to ensure top quality furniture at bargain prices, and checklists to make sure that none of the important steps are forgotten. Finally, we will work together to get your property listed on all of the portals, and ensure your listings are optimised to get as many bookings as possible from day one! If you feel that this service would be of value to you, please send her an email at <u>peaceproperty@yahoo.co.uk</u>

Join a Mastermind Group

Are the right people surrounding you to accelerate your path to success? We will create plans for you to work through the obstacles that may stand in our way and achieve your goals. We will all inspire and encourage each other on our set goals. Many of the world's greatest entrepreneurs like Richard Branson openly admit that they wouldn't be where they are today without their mentors.

If you've started your serviced accommodation business and you are looking to systemise and scale your business, then my mastermind group may be the "fast-forward" your business is looking for.

This mastermind group is structured as monthly meetings, with each meeting covering an agenda which includes progress updates, pain points, a deal clinic and learning focused on specific topics. To ensure you are staying on track, and to deal with any issues that might have arisen in the meantime. If you would like to discuss this opportunity further, please email peaceproperty@yahoo.co.uk

Giving Back

Blessed Hill Children's Centre is an organization designed to support, educate, feed and house orphaned, abandoned and rejected children in Uganda. In 2016, I had the chance to visit this orphanage and I witnessed their daily struggles. My dream is to support this orphanage by establishing a bakery which will enable children to learn the life skill of baking. It is my hope that this will promote their economic independence and empowerment for them to become people of value when they leave the orphanage.

For every copy of this book sold, I will be donating £1 towards the building project of a bakery and all the facilities needed for it to function properly. If you wish to discuss this opportunity further, please email and together we can make a difference to the orphans living in Uganda.

ABOUT THE AUTHOR

Julian Businge is a mother, wife, author, entrepreneur and international speaker. She is the Managing Director of Peace Apartments: a leading provider of Serviced Accommodation in England, UK. She is also a CEO of Peace Property Education: an emerging provider of property education. She has a wider experience in managing serviced accommodation and offers coaching to those who wish to start their businesses.